A PROCESS FOR TRANSFORMING
LEARNING INTO PERFORMANCE

THE FOUR MOMENTS *of* TRUTH

D1104718

Sam K. Shriver Ed.D.

Foreword by James D. Kirkpatrick and Wendy Kayser Kirkpatrick
Afterword by Doug Harward

THE CENTER FOR LEADERSHIP STUDIES

The Four Moments of Truth is published by:

Leadership Studies, Inc. dba The Center for Leadership Studies.
280 Towerview Court
Cary, NC 27513
(919) 335-8763

Printed in the United States of America
Leadership Studies, Inc. © 2018

ISBN 978-0-931619-12-0

For information about permission to reproduce selections from this
book, email permissions@situational.com.

For more information, visit www.situational.com.

To coach William Rayl of the El Segundo Eagles

a true master at connecting *training* to *practice*
and *practice* to *performance* under the umbrella
of all that is *coaching*.

Acknowledgments

First and foremost, I feel it is important to acknowledge my wife and the CEO of The Center for Leadership Studies. Suffice it to say that I have no idea what my life would have been like without Maureen Hersey Shriver and will spend no time whatsoever contemplating that comparatively dismal alternative! Sincere thanks ... for all ... and I love you.

Second, I spent the better part of a quarter century designing, developing, delivering and evaluating the impact of hundreds of custom training programs. These offerings were primarily focused on leadership development. I have no idea what that journey would have looked like without Jim Phelan and John Nasser. Both provided opportunities to do cutting-edge work on high-visibility projects that forced our team to stay current, be creative and stretch. Duane McDaniel, who worked with John years ago, provided ground-floor insight into what would eventually become The Four Moments of Truth™.

Third, there comes a time during the process of a project such as writing a book when you think you are finished. So, you ask a trusted colleague or two to review it for you and find out you are not! Such was the case with an early draft of this treatise. Ken Taylor and Michelle Eggleston at Training Industry, Inc. provided actionable feedback on an early draft that I believe greatly improved what you are about to consume.

Finally, I would like to call out the contributions of Maria Dalmolin. Maria is a Senior Performance Consultant and Instructional Designer with The Center for Leadership Studies. Simply stated, Maria is a master of her craft. She is consistently creative, meticulous, relentless and fun. She has contributed so much to so many projects over the years. This book, and the materials that put its message into action, are but the most recent of her contributions of significance.

Contents

Foreword

James D. Kirkpatrick and Wendy Kayser Kirkpatrick
Coauthors, "Kirkpatrick's Four Levels of Training Evaluation"

Sam Shriver and the team at The Center for Leadership Studies (CLS) put forth a humble statement in Chapter 1 of this valuable book; it contains no new ideas. This statement is perhaps overly modest. *"The Four Moments of Truth"* provides an easy-to-understand framework for making training work in today's workplace. The moments of truth are founded on and supported by decades of research and implementation by training industry trailblazers and leaders. This background is also succinctly and simply stated for every learning professional to quickly understand.

So, why another book on the importance of focusing on what happens after training? Quite simply because organizations are not doing it. Sadly, the research continues to show that a small fraction of what is learned in training is used on the job. So, even the most excellent, well-conceived training has little chance of contributing to organizational results.

While this book is targeted to training professionals, it is important to share it with business leaders at all levels because they are part of the perpetual problem. Many training professionals will eagerly read this book and nod their heads in agreement, thinking, "I know. If only I could engage people in the business to do their part after training." I hope business leaders will read this book with as much interest as I predict training professionals will.

With all due respect to the training industry and other business functions it serves, it is time for the cycle of waste to end. Let this be the decade in history when training and the business unite and accept the reality that training in and of itself is a consumer of resources, not a contributor to outcomes. The contributions come from a work environment that nurtures implementation of good practices that yield the desired results. This work environment is built through the system of support and accountability Sam describes in this book.

We are grateful that he has put forward the Kirkpatrick Model as the foundation of workplace training and performance success. The Four Moments of Truth™ beautifully complement it. We are impressed by the level of dedication Sam and the CLS team show in championing a better way to do business through targeted training and multifaceted support and follow-up. We hope this book will be the tipping point to change the way training and business are done.

On a more personal note, we have known and worked with Sam and some of his colleagues for 10 years. What we have learned from our many interactions together is that this book is more than principles and techniques. Sam and his colleagues have woven their core values of training, work and quality of life within and between the lines. His organization is fully committed to doing what they can to uncover and maximize the power of the human spirit. Yes, much of what is presented can be automated, but the results come largely from people working together to bring the technology, and the principles of the model, to vibrant success.

Read and enjoy this book and share it with whomever is on the other side of the proverbial fence in your organization. Discuss how to apply these ideas and select a pilot program to try it out. Many people we encounter seem daunted by the idea of trying something new, especially when it represents a cultural change. A single pilot reduces risk and fear and creates a wonderful incubator to test new ideas. We sincerely hope you give this approach a try.

About This Book

This book is about sustainment, training transfer and behavior change. It is intended to serve as a practical guidebook for anyone with a vested interest in positively impacting performance through training.

As we are all very much aware, event-based training is rapidly going the way of the dinosaur. An engaging event is still an important piece of the sustainment puzzle, of course, but it is no longer the only piece that bears strategic consideration. Training that moves the needle on performance is a function of an integrated process. That process is dependent upon several key stakeholders understanding and executing their roles in an effort to connect learning to tangible, real-world achievement.

Each of the following chapters features a mix of storytelling, explanation and user-friendly guidance to present our Four Moments of Truth™ sustainment process. This process is firmly grounded in industry-standard research from experts in the fields of training, evaluation and the link between behavior change and targeted achievement.

When effectively employed in conjunction with Situational Leadership® training (or for that matter, any training whatsoever), the Four Moments of Truth guarantees results! If that sounds like an over-the-top, attention-grabbing, audacious claim, so be it. We stand behind it because it accurately represents our direct experiences with customers large and small at The Center for Leadership Studies (CLS).

And, if you are unfamiliar with Situational Leadership®, CLS or both, I offer the following list of terms in an effort to provide additional grounding on the vantage point that frames my perspective of authorship:

Situational Leadership® – A leadership model that has been used to train over 14 million leaders worldwide

Dr. Paul Hersey – The "father" of Situational Leadership® and the founder of The Center for Leadership Studies

The Center for Leadership Studies (CLS) – The global home of Situational Leadership® founded by Dr. Hersey in 1969

The Four Moments of Truth™ **(4MOT**™**)** – A process developed over time by many at CLS and in active partnership with our customers to effectively sustain Situational Leadership® training

Pronouns "I," "We" and "Our" – used interchangeably throughout this text as a reflection of the current views of "Team CLS"

THE FOUR
MOMENTS
of TRUTH

CHAPTER 1

I'm Just Trying to Matter!

I was sitting in a movie theatre when I first heard that line. It was a response delivered by Academy Award-winning actress Reese Witherspoon in the film *"Walk the Line."* As at least some (and perhaps many) may remember, the movie chronicled the rise of country-western star Johnny Cash and his romantic pursuit of fellow performer June Carter (played by Reese Witherspoon). In an attention-grabbing exchange between the two that could best be described as highly emotional, Cash confronts Carter and asks:

"June, just what are you trying to do?"

Without missing a beat, Carter reflects on the overwhelming number of personal and professional forces that are actively competing for her attention at that moment and responds by saying:

"I'm just trying to matter!"

I remember thinking at the time, "What a great line! How simple! How profound! What a perfect way to encapsulate what June (and just about everybody) is trying to get out of life." We simply want to matter. As learning professionals, our stage is a classroom, be it physical or virtual, and the value we have the potential to provide rests within each learner we encounter. Can we, through the content we deliver, ignite a spark that turns into a flame and burns brightly long after the event has concluded? That's how we matter! We play a role in helping others build transferable skills that will make a discernible difference in the worlds from which they came. Therefore, with the exploits of Johnny and June as a backdrop, I offer our Four Moments of Truth™ (4MOT™) as your road map for "mattering." It is a simple, practical process that Trainers, Trainees and the Next-Level Managers (NLMs) of those Trainees can employ to tangibly transform what is learned to what is accomplished on the job.

Consider each moment in the 4MOT as a critical juncture on a well-established pathway, where the integrated alignment of the Trainer, Trainee and NLM determines the impact of training on performance. As you will discover, 4MOT is a time-sensitive process that is grounded in the contributions of the following thought leaders: Donald, James and Wendy Kirkpatrick; Mary Broad and John Newstrom; Robert Brinkerhoff; Anders Ericsson and Dr. Paul Hersey.

Chapter 2 and Chapter 5 will provide background and some detail on the specific contributions of each, but for now, here is a high-level overview of the 4MOT process.

Introduction to the 4MOT™

To set the stage for our exploration, I would ask you to adopt a philosophical perspective of training as a personalized change initiative. It's a journey that initiates with fundamental exposure and culminates with demonstrated expertise. I would readily acknowledge that the true duration of any journey dedicated to skill-set mastery would be more accurately depicted as "a lifelong expedition." But, for our purposes, we'll focus on a period of concentrated analysis of between 6 and 18 months (i.e., the journey begins with a training experience, which serves as the catalyst for behavior change that produces tangible results over that period of time).

To begin, let's define the three key stakeholders who will command our focused attention.

4MOT Three Key Stakeholders

The Trainer

This includes not only the person delivering the live or virtual message of the training, but also all who have played a role in designing and developing the experience. If the training isn't both relevant and engaging, the probability of transfer is substantially decreased.

The Trainee
This is the individual who will engage with the formal learning directly and then attempt to implement what was learned in a real-world setting for the express purpose of delivering targeted results.

The Next-Level Manager (NLM)
This is the immediate supervisor or manager of the Trainee on the learning journey. The NLM has been proven (by the sources we have identified and many others) to be the single most important driver of training transfer. In that regard, consider the NLM as a "light switch" of sorts. Assuming the formal learning experience is of high quality, the NLM can almost single-handedly turn on the switch, effectively facilitating application for results that truly matter, or turn off the switch, essentially eliminating any reasonable probability that the Trainee will practice what has been preached.

Given those three key stakeholders, the 4MOT delivers a process that ensures the NLM supports Trainees at critical moments in the learning cycle to both position and reinforce the training event.

The Four Moments of Truth™
Each moment of truth will be explored in detail in this book, but here is a brief overview.

Same-Page Status	Maximum Engagement	Perfect Practice	Performance Support
MOT1	MOT2	MOT3	MOT4
Outline Training Expectations One to Two Weeks Before Training	During Training	Post-Training Coaching One to Two Weeks After Training	Ongoing Coaching Three Months After Training
Pre-Training	During	Post-Training	Ongoing

MOT1: Same-Page Status

The NLM and the Trainee negotiate expectations for learning during formal training. In particular, that exchange addresses how the learning has the potential to be applied (post-training) in a manner that can positively impact productivity, engagement and perhaps even retention. The focus is on aligned expectations to include a follow-up discussion on what was learned and how it can be applied (MOT3).

MOT2: Maximum Engagement

This defines the roles of the NLM and Trainee during formal learning. Both have distinctly different responsibilities.

MOT3: Perfect Practice

In many ways, MOT3 (the first post-training discussion between the Trainee and NLM) is the most critical. Not surprisingly, it relies heavily on a well-executed MOT1 and MOT2.

MOT4: Performance Support

This is the point in time at which coaching discussions targeting what was learned in training blend into natural, normal, ongoing performance coaching.

As you contemplate turning another page or two, allow me to conclude this introduction by acknowledging the following: there are very few (if any) original thoughts in this book!

Perhaps that seems like a strange admission, but I assure you it is both accurate and intended. The value in investing another minute of your time to understand 4MOT lies in the potential benefits you stand to gain from a more in-depth appreciation of a practical, user-friendly sustainment process that compiles the significant insight and analysis of others. Those contributors will be featured with profound respect in Chapter 2.

Chapter 1: Key Takeaway

Those of us who find ourselves in the training industry are really no different than anyone else; we simply want to matter! We seek meaning in life by helping others develop skills and produce results that play some discernible role in their organization's viability and competitive standing.

A Brief History of Learning and Performance

Learning, in one form or another, has been on active display since the beginning of time. Let's pick up our review of that journey in the 1950s. That was the general time frame when organizations began formally establishing functions and departments dedicated to the discipline. Not so coincidentally, it also marks the point in time when a true training industry giant quietly emerged onto the scene.

Kirkpatrick's Four Levels

It is difficult to imagine where our profession would be without Dr. Donald Kirkpatrick. He was the undisputed pioneer of evaluation science in adult learning and a beloved ambassador of all things training. As I understand the backdrop to the beginning of the Kirkpatrick story, he was pursuing his doctorate from the University of Wisconsin in the mid-1950s. His dissertation was about measuring the impact of a supervisory training program, and, at the time, his circumstances required him to figure out what form that measurement would take. He kept things simple, which no doubt contributed greatly to the eventual popularity of the framework for which he has been credited:

Level 1: Reaction – The degree to which participants find the training favorable, engaging and relevant to their jobs

Level 2: Learning – The degree to which participants acquire the intended knowledge, skills, attitude, confidence and commitment based on their participation in the training

8

Level 3: Behavior – The degree to which participants apply what they learned during training when they are back on the job

Level 4: Results – The degree to which targeted outcomes occur as a result of the training and the support and accountability package

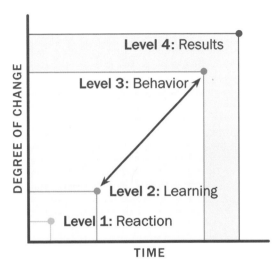

Figure 1: The degree of change between learning and behavior. (Adapted from: Kirkpatrick JD, Kirkpatrick WK. Kirkpatrick's Four Levels of Training Evaluation. Arlington, VA: ATD Press; 2016.)

Not long after Dr. Kirkpatrick completed his degree requirements, he was contacted by a newly formed organization called the American Society for Training & Development (currently the Association for Talent Development [ATD]). They had come across his dissertation, and they asked if he would publish an article grounded in his findings in one of their first publications in the late 1950s. He wrote a series of four articles entitled "Reaction," "Learning," "Behavior" and "Results." The rest, as they say, is history.

The Kirkpatrick Model (or some variation of it) became the established standard that learning and development professionals used to measure the impact of a wide spectrum of training experiences. To be fair, a much more accurate statement would be that Level 1 of Kirkpatrick's four levels became the established standard. Unfortunately, most organizations stopped there.

The cruel, cold reality associated with measuring training outcomes beyond the workshop experience was that few organizations even bothered. This was particularly the case for training dedicated to topics such as leadership, influence and change management. As it applies to actual measurement for training in that realm, the endeavor could best be described as a well-intended leap of faith.

There was defendable logic that governed that position. First, the misconception abounded that Level 2 is only evaluated with a formal pre-test and post-test. Second, the costs associated with the ill-conceived idea that isolating all the variables is necessary to effectively measure the true impact of a two-day leadership workshop simply did not add up:

"We're not in the measurement or assessment business; we're in the (fill in the blank) business!"

There was also rationale based on a different, but admittedly valid, observation that resulted in similar reticence to rigorously measure Level 2 outcomes. In paraphrased form, it went something like this:

> "It flies in the face of everything we are coming to recognize and understand about adult learning principles. The idea of administering a pre-test to employees expressly designed to document a baseline for learning that we intuitively know already exists is insulting. If recently promoted managers have not previously attended Situational Leadership® training, it stands to reason they wouldn't know the meaning of terms like Performance Readiness®, task behavior, relationship behavior, etc., let alone how framing leadership opportunities in the context of those terms could increase their effectiveness as leaders. We are not dealing with elementary school students required to take standardized tests at the beginning and end of a school year as a mechanism to

justify a recommendation for advancement. Pre-tests and post-tests in adult learning are borderline offensive and, as such, diminish the probability of achieving the outcomes you are attempting to achieve."

As a result, and in overwhelming unison, many organizations began confining their evaluation efforts of human skills training to Level 1 measures. They would track metrics such as the number of courses offered, the number of participants in attendance and how those learners felt about the training facilities, the facilitator, the course itself and their intentions to implement what they learned when they returned to their jobs. Data that connected an organization's investment in leadership training to true measures of productivity were rare. Even still, in the mid-1980s, additional research under the umbrella of "training evaluation" was taking a new tack. Given the general acceptance of Kirkpatrick's four levels, why wasn't there more evidence of behavior change that resulted in documented impact?

Manager Role in Training Transfer

From our perspective, no research in this context provided better commonsense insight than the work of Mary Broad and John Newstrom. The premise of their contributions was both inquisitive and practical:

> "If we agree that Kirkpatrick's four levels framework includes the spectrum of outcomes we have the potential to measure relative to training, why aren't there significantly more Level 3 and Level 4 results?"

They framed their inquiry by forming a matrix that visually represented the predictable time periods that define training in a very general sense, with an equally general description of the primary stakeholders, each of whom has a role in the dynamics of training transfer.

The questions that guided their research formed a crossroads defined by "looking back and looking forward." Given a stated objective of training transfer (e.g., what is learned in training will be implemented on the job), consider the matrix in Figure 2a, and answer the following questions:

1. What role/time combination(s) most accurately identify traditional responsibility for training transfer (i.e., which stakeholder[s] in which time period[s] have had primary responsibility for training transfer)?

2. What role/time combination(s) should be responsible (i.e., which stakeholder[s] in which time period[s] truly drive Level 3 and Level 4 outcomes)?

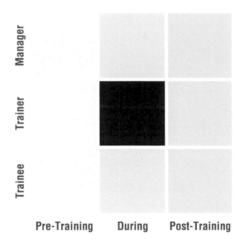

Figure 2a: The Transfer Matrix. (Adapted from: Broad ML, Newstrom JW, Transfer of Training: Action Packed Strategies to Ensure High Payoff From Training Investments. Perseus Publishing; 1992.)

To the surprise of absolutely no one, the Trainer during training was the clear answer to the first question. If you have ever seen (or for that matter, been) a Trainer at the end of a workshop literally begging participants to use the skills they just learned as they walk out the door after receiving their certificates, you know exactly what I am talking about! In reality, the minute learners leave the confines of training, they transition back into a world that is most significantly influenced by their NLM.

As such, it should come as no surprise that the answer Broad and Newstrom uncovered to the second question is that the NLM, before and after training, is the key driver of Level 3 and Level 4 outcomes. If you are truly interested in Trainees retaining learning, changing their behavior and applying what they learned on the job, the stakeholder that has the most potential to make that happen is the person responsible for the Trainee's output in a real-world setting — the NLM.

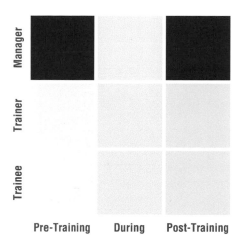

Figure 2b: The Transfer Matrix. (Adapted from: Broad ML, Newstrom JW, Transfer of Training: Action Packed Strategies to Ensure High Payoff From Training Investments. Perseus Publishing; 1992.)

Helping and Hindering Roles
The contributions of Broad and Newstrom (and several others conducting similar research) were not lost on Dr. Kirkpatrick. In light of these developments, he identified a continuum of helping and hindering roles that NLMs have the potential to play pertaining to the task of training transfer. Consider the following hypothetical comments as examples of what each NLM might sound like in discussion with a Trainee prior to an upcoming learning event.

Preventing

"So, as I understand it, you're not going to be here next week because you have to attend training. Personal opinion: you're going to learn absolutely nothing of value, and this simply couldn't be happening at a worse time. Keep your phone on and close by because I know we are going to have questions that only you can answer."

Discouraging

"If you learn something useful in that class, I will be blown away."

Neutral

"You're in training next week, right? Just to confirm, you are going to be out on Wednesday and Thursday, correct? OK, thanks."

Encouraging

"You know, when I look back on it, I really enjoyed that course and felt it had a lot to do with shaping who I became as a manager. If it makes sense to discuss that a little more when you return to work, be sure to let me know. I really think you are going to get a lot out of the experience."

Requiring

"I want to make sure the two of us get some time together before you attend training next week. This kind of experience can have a dramatic impact on your effectiveness. It's important that you and I are on the same page as it applies to the training itself, and my expectation is that you put together a plan to use what you learned when you get back. I will set up a time for us to discuss that plan in detail."

Level	Manager Support	Outcome
PREVENTING	Manager sees training as being in direct opposition to their style	Training does not transfer
DISCOURAGING	Manager sends negative message about the skills learned in training by modeling contradictory behaviors in the workplace	Training does not transfer
NEUTRAL	Manager ignores training and adopts business-as-usual attitude	Learner decides whether or not to implement training as manager neither objects to nor supports it
ENCOURAGING	Manager encourages employee to put training into action by showing interest in what was learned	Training is likely to transfer
REQUIRING	Manager knows what was learned and insists on implementation — in some cases creating contracts to ensure implementation	Training will be implemented

Figure 3: Helping and hindering roles. (Adapted from: Kirkpatrick DL, Kirkpatrick JD. Evaluating Training Programs: The Four Levels. 3rd ed. San Francisco, CA: Berrett-Koehler Publishers, Inc.; 2006.)

In terms all can understand at a glance, Robert Brinkerhoff confirmed the impact of a Requiring Manager on Level 3 and Level 4 outcomes. In research he conducted with Anne Apking, Dr. Brinkerhoff found that the direct involvement of a Requiring Manager in the time periods identified in Figure 4 could increase levels of learner retention by as much as 65 percent.

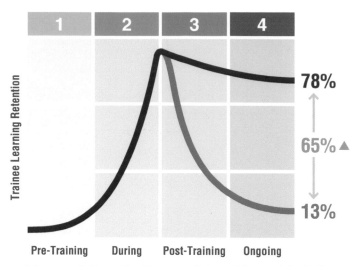

Figure 4: Impact of a Requiring Manager. (Adapted from Brinkerhoff RO, Apking AM. High Impact Learning: New Perspectives in Organizational Learning, Performance, and Change. Cambridge, MA: Perseus; 2001.)

Consider that change and the difference between the limits established in Figure 4 (i.e., 13 percent retention versus 78 percent). You sign up for (or are required to attend) training. You receive some pre-training notices from the provider covering logistics, objectives and perhaps even some pre-work. In all likelihood, it would never occur to you to discuss the training or review this material with your NLM unless they initiated the conversation. So, you would show up to the designated place at the required time for the training event. During participant introductions at the beginning of the program, you might say something like:

"I'm just here to learn about leadership and hopefully improve as a result."

Let us further assume the training is highly engaging and relevant. You complete the end-of-workshop Level 1 evaluation and rate everything either a "4" or a "5" on the scale provided. The instructor, in particular, was outstanding. You emerge from training with a high level of commitment to practice what has been preached and have a documented Action Plan to do so.

What Brinkerhoff is suggesting in Figure 4 is that without the engagement of a Requiring Manager who knows what you learned and plans to hold you accountable for integrated application, Level 3 outcomes would be rare. For example, if you were randomly selected three months or so after you emerged from training and asked to discuss the impact of the training experience with Dr. Brinkerhoff, that discussion might unfold something like this:

> **Dr. Brinkerhoff:** "You attended the Situational Leadership® training last quarter. Tell me a little bit about what you learned."
>
> **You:** "I remember I thought it was a great course with a very strong facilitator. The model itself is common sense."
>
> **Dr. Brinkerhoff:** "Common sense?"
>
> **You:** "Yeah, sometimes as a leader you need to be 'hands-on'; other times you need to 'talk things over'; and occasionally you need to take more of a 'hands-off' approach. It all depends."
>
> **Dr. Brinkerhoff:** "Depends on what?"
>
> **You:** "Well, any number of things really."

If that sounds familiar, you can relate to the impact. Whether your manager was encouraging, preventing, discouraging or neutral, the takeaway is that their behavior presented a barrier to your ability to apply what you learned.

Now, consider what this pre-training scenario would look like if your NLM intentionally played the role of a Requiring Manager. The two of you spend focused time discussing why the training is important and what you hope to gain from the experience. In general terms, your NLM communicates the potential impact the upcoming training could have on opportunities and challenges your group is experiencing. He or she also assures you that during training:

"... the rest of us will fill in as needed to make sure everything is covered while you are away ... your job is to get as much as you can possibly get out of the experience, and be prepared to tell me what you learned and how you plan to put that learning to use to the benefit of your team when you return."

It simply stands to reason you would enter training with a different mindset based on your NLM's proactive involvement. As a result, your participant introduction during training might sound something like this:

"I am a new manager of a seasoned and highly productive team that has been together for a while. We are about to implement a significant process change, so I want to learn how to lead my team successfully through the change. I also want to be able to build credibility in the process because they know much more about the technical aspects of their jobs than I do."

Assuming your NLM followed through and had a post-training discussion that pinpointed the manner in which you were going to implement what you learned, how that would be measured and what role the NLM would play in helping you achieve those results, your discussion with Dr. Brinkerhoff three months after training would probably sound a lot different as well:

Dr. Brinkerhoff: "You attended Situational Leadership® training last quarter. Tell me a little bit about what you learned."

You: "In a nutshell, that program changed the way I manage people."

Dr. Brinkerhoff: "How so?"

You: "I think the main reason was that it taught me how to approach leading people in a much more objective manner. There are basically four steps to

Situational Leadership®: identify a specific task; assess the Performance Readiness® of the individual you are attempting to influence to perform that task; match your style or leadership approach to that level of readiness; and understand that your fundamental role as a manager is to accelerate the development of people on your team and redirect any performance-related regression that takes place over time. I think through those steps just about every time I have the opportunity to influence anyone."

Dr. Brinkerhoff: "Can you give me a specific example?"

You: "Sure. When I attended the training, we were on the brink of introducing a significant process change which would directly impact my team — a very tenured group that liked things the way they were. By definition, that translated to low levels of Performance Readiness® for the tasks I was going to ask the members on my team to complete. The 'WHAT' they were doing would remain generally the same, but the 'HOW' was going to be very different. I needed to become comfortable quickly with the leader-driven approaches (style 1 and style 2) in an effort to create movement in the right direction. For what it's worth, that was by no means my comfort zone! Initially, my manager really helped me. We role-played quite a bit and discussed influence approaches for each member of my team for different tasks. One thing that really resonated with me was ..."

Bottom line, it is difficult to imagine that somebody could consistently apply something they learned in training on the job if they are struggling to remember anything specific about the training itself. Stated a different way, learning does not automatically translate to behavior change, but behavior change initiated by learning does translate to increased understanding. The change in retention levels shown in Figure 4 is a product of application driven by NLM reinforcement over time. In that regard, and in full acknowledgment of all the variables that impact the outcomes of every learning event, I would offer that no variable is more critical than the active integration of the Trainee's NLM.

Leader Effectiveness

It is similar to an equation Dr. Hersey used to address the relative importance of the many variables that determine a leader's degree of effectiveness:

$$Le = f (s, f, b, a, c, p, e, etc.)$$

(Leader effectiveness is a function of the situation, the follower, the leader's boss, the leader's associates/peers, the culture of the organization, the performance of the organization, the economy and many other situational factors.)

In his paraphrased words, "... all of these variables are important, of course, but if the follower decides not to follow, it doesn't matter what your boss or your associates think, what the culture of your organization is, how well your company is performing, how well the economy is doing, etc."

Much the same applies to "training effectiveness" defined by behavior change on the job that produces targeted results. A number of variables come into play, of course, but none transcends the direct and intentional involvement of the NLM.

$$Te = f (t, nlm, tm, c, p, e, etc.)$$

(Training effectiveness is a function of the training [to include the effectiveness of the delivery and the active engagement of the Trainee], the next-level manager, top management support, the culture of the organization, the performance of the organization, the economy, etc.)

Without a relevant training experience and an NLM who acts as a catalyst for transfer, training effectiveness becomes more of a random occurrence than a predictable and repeatable outcome.

Learning as Change

All of this brings us full circle and back to Kirkpatrick. The four levels remain the single most visible and useful evaluation framework in our industry. As a graduate of the Kirkpatrick bronze level certification program, I find that the recent contributions of James and Wendy Kirkpatrick have taken a good thing and made it significantly better. The original Kirkpatrick Model was frequently interpreted starting from the bottom and working up (i.e., design training that will teach learners something to which they will respond favorably [Reaction], and then see if they apply what they learned [Behavior] and if it makes any difference [Results]). The tactical journey for the Trainee remains a bottom-up progression, but the strategy that charts the course for that expedition leverages training as a streamlined change initiative that is all about achieving targeted outcomes. In James Kirkpatrick's words, "… you need to start with the flag at the top of the mountain and work your way down."

Here is a series of questions to answer if you plan to embed learning into the achievement of relevant organizational goals:

1. What are our key strategic initiatives?

    a. How can training help us achieve the objectives dictated by our strategy?

2. If employees implemented what they learned in training, what would be different (i.e., behaviorally, what would they start doing, stop doing or do more of)?

    a. What can we do to accelerate that behavior change and get the most out of our investment in training?

3. How do we teach employees what they need to know in an engaging manner?

    a. How much time will it take to transfer that learning and produce documented results?

CLS developed the 4MOT™ primarily to help organizations answer Question 2a. Of course, NLMs are busy with any number of competing priorities, but the next four chapters will detail a process that, if followed, guarantees the transfer of well-designed training.

Chapter 2: Key Takeaway

The 4MOT primarily serves as the practical integration of foundational transfer of training contributions made by the Kirkpatricks, Broad and Newstrom and Brinkerhoff. If nothing else, it firmly establishes the critical role the NLM plays in translating newfound Trainee understanding and learning into measurable behavioral change.

CHAPTER 3

MOT1: Same-Page Status

So many things in life are simple to understand, yet very difficult to do. Consider leadership as an example. Have you ever read about a high-profile leader "communicating transparently" or "actively listening" or "practicing what they preach" and found yourself thinking something like, "Thank you, Captain Obvious?" In large part, great leaders accomplish feats of significance by figuring out a way to turn common sense into common practice.

It's much the same with training transfer or sustainment. Chapter 2 advanced the premise that many variables exist that drive or contribute to behavior change, with none being more important than the dedicated involvement of the NLM. By virtue of their legitimate power (i.e., ability to reward, sanction and make decisions), NLMs can significantly influence the priorities (and, as such, the behavior) of those within the formal span of their control. Assuming the employee in question has aspirations of upward mobility, or at least of ongoing employment in good standing, the NLM is a natural and powerful accelerator for

Key Questions
- Do you really expect every NLM to engage in a MOT1 discussion with every direct report attending formal learning? (Spoiler alert: yes!)

- How much time does an NLM need to invest to effectively drive a MOT1 discussion? (If properly structured, far less than you might think!)

23

any number of developmental opportunities. In that sense, the dynamics bear at least partial similarity to a parent dedicated to the prospect of ensuring their offspring maximizes their potential, and a child who can periodically be distracted by any number of "shiny objects" on the road to maturity.

In that regard, put your political affiliation aside for a moment — admittedly easier said than done — and consider the documented history of Dr. Ben Carson and his mother, Sonya, as an illustration of that dynamic. In the best-selling book *"Gifted Hands,"* Dr. Carson chronicles the approach his mother took with his primary and secondary education. The first step was a conversation she had with his teachers every year regarding what was being taught, why it was important and what she could do to ensure young Ben stayed on track. Now, we have to assume, given the fact that she was a single parent working two (and sometimes three) jobs, that these conversations were structured, to the point and not overly time-consuming. We also have to assume that Mrs. Carson's voluntary time investment communicated at least a couple of things to the younger Carson, as well as his teachers:

1. "I care about this. The education of my son is important to me."

2. "We are in this together. You have the day watch. I have the night watch. Let's do this thing!"

Mrs. Carson's night watch duties included several well-documented sustainment strategies. She discussed, in no uncertain terms, her expectations for Ben when he went to school. He was going to pay attention, he was going to learn and he was going to achieve his potential regardless of what anyone else was doing. To measure the progress associated with that journey, Mrs. Carson instituted what anyone in the education and training business would have to agree was a brilliant short-term follow-up strategy: the twice-a-week essay.

Each week, above and beyond the assigned homework that Ben received from school, he needed to draft and read aloud two essays that covered what he was in the process of learning. The essays needed to include perspective on why that learning might be important and how he might be able to use or apply what he was learning. Before young Ben could do what he wanted with his discretionary time, he had to draft and articulate these assigned essays to Mrs. Carson's satisfaction. In Kirkpatrick terms, this would be the epitome of a Requiring Manager.

Now, implementing this plan probably came with its share of obstacles (lack of sleep, not enough time in the day, adolescent kid you love more than life itself trying like crazy to convince you that this is a bad idea, etc.). But, through it all, Sonya Carson stuck with the plan. Ultimately, she figured out a way to take her strategy to the next level. She began following up with Ben on the intentions he had expressed to apply what he learned, adding a level of accountability to his development.

There are truly so many things all of us can learn from the Sonya Carsons of the world, and, as it applies to the transfer and/or sustainment of education and training, I would suggest none is more important than the proactive impact an NLM (or a dedicated parent) can have on an educational outcome. If Trainees clearly understand that they will be expected not only to learn something useful, but also to create a strategic document that reviews what they learned, how they plan to implement that learning on the job and the projected impact that applied knowledge could have on productivity, it stands to reason that they will approach the learning event with an orientation toward action and achievement, as opposed to "box checking" and completion.

Are there obstacles that get in the way of all this? You bet! Chief among them are the time demands placed on managers to handle all sorts of other important duties. That being the case, is it realistic to think that managers have the bandwidth to get completely up to speed with everything their employees are going to be learning for each and every course they attend to effectively conduct a pre-training coaching session during MOT1? Of course not. Sonya Carson was nowhere near "the weeds" of everything young Ben was learning in every class every day he was in school — what single parent working multiple jobs could be? She did, however, know which classes he was taking, the general instructional intent of those offerings and how that knowledge could contribute to Ben becoming more productive as a student in the midst of his ongoing journey to fulfill his potential. With the Ben Carson story in mind, the 4MOT™ features materials for the Trainee and NLM that are intended to provide the structure necessary for the Trainee to draft and articulate a course-specific, twice-a-week essay.

Roles in Moment of Truth 1 (MOT1)

MOT1 is a function of interdependence. Both the Trainee and the NLM are required to engage in a thoughtful review of the training objectives and job requirements, as well as a proactive consideration of how applying what is about to be learned could make a positive difference in productivity. MOT1 sets the stage for a journey that integrates learning with behavior change and behavior change with measurable progress.

The 4MOT process is time-sensitive. In the excerpt below, the NLM receives the following specific direction regarding their role in MOT1:

DIRECTIONS

☐ Prior to this meeting, the Trainee should review the program overview and learning objectives and be prepared to discuss how the content is relevant to their role.

☐ Discuss how the program content relates to the Trainee's performance, and explore what they hope to gain from the training.

☐ Engage with the Trainee to identify developmental opportunities.

☐ Agree upon two to three training-related objectives.

The actions expected of the Trainee for MOT1 include:

DIRECTIONS

☐ Review the program overview and learning objectives prior to meeting with your NLM.

☐ Discuss what you hope to gain from the training with your NLM and identify developmental opportunities.

☐ Agree upon two to three training-related objectives.

It's important to spend a little more time addressing the primary obstacle to the real-world implementation of the 4MOT: "Our managers are overloaded as it is."

Candidly, comments like these strike us as odd, particularly for organizations that contend they need to see a return on their training investment and are absolutely committed to providing training that produces behavior change. Even still, we cannot argue with the reality that NLMs in organizations around the world are not sitting idly by and looking for ways to pass the time. They are indeed busy! They are frequently overworked! And, their time is certainly at a premium!

In full acknowledgment of these realities, I would ask you to participate in a quick and highly personalized research project. Open the stopwatch function on your mobile phone, hit "start" and read the content in the graphic below.

Situational Leadership®: Building Leaders

Program Overview

Situational Leadership®: Building Leaders equips leaders in organizations with the tools necessary to skillfully navigate the demands of an increasingly diverse workforce and evolving global marketplace. Widely adaptable to any circumstance, Situational Leadership® provides participants with an action-oriented leadership framework that increases both the quantity and quality of performance discussions.

Through a combination of training, role-playing and skill-building activities, the *Situational Leadership®: Building Leaders* program provides ample opportunity to practice applying the core tenets of the model. Participants learn to effectively influence by matching an individual's Performance Readiness® Level for a specific task with the appropriate leadership style. Participants learn how to assess and adapt to effectively manage the opportunities and challenges associated with leading others.

In addition, online or paper-based assessments (LEAD Self and LEAD Other) provide participants with insights into their primary and secondary leadership styles to understand how their own behavioral preferences could impact their ability to diagnose Performance Readiness® and respond with a matching leadership style. Participants leverage this awareness of their behavioral tendencies to explore their current leadership strengths and identify areas where there is room for improvement.

Objectives

Upon completion of this program, participants should be able to:

▸ Define leadership

▸ Apply Situational Leadership® by:
  – Identifying the specific task
  – Accurately assessing an individual's Performance Readiness® to perform a specific task
  – Responding with the right leadership style and behaviors to meet the performance needs of the individual
  – Communicating the leader response more effectively
  – Managing the movement of the individual through various levels of Performance Readiness®

▸ Identify opportunities to improve through self-assessment and development planning

Situational Leadership®: Building Leaders course overview.

Think Sonya Carson here. We would suggest that the time it took you to read the program information you just read, with a few minutes added in for reflection, is a good approximation of the required commitment an NLM would need to effectively prepare for a MOT1 discussion with a direct report scheduled to attend an upcoming training event.

The MOT1 Discussion

The objectives for the MOT1 discussion are as follows:

1. Prepare the Trainee to engage as an active participant in the training event they are about to experience.

2. Ensure the Trainee that during training (MOT2), their work-related priority is to do all they can to engage in the training, learn and prepare for MOT3.

3. Communicate clear expectations regarding your intentions to follow up with the Trainee in MOT3 one to two weeks after training to discuss:

    a. What they learned

    b. How they plan to implement that knowledge

    c. The role the NLM should play in helping to implement the plan

    d. The projected impact of that behavior change on productivity (i.e., sales, morale, retention, efficiency, etc.)

In short, a Ben Carson twice-a-week essay. From our experience, these MOT1 discussions are also extremely time efficient, taking only about 15 minutes. And, while there is no way to choreograph a specific and repeatable flow for each discussion, we'd like to offer the following suggestions:

In the language of Situational Leadership®, this is an S2 to S3 exchange (think "explanation, discussion and collaboration").

The NLM should:

1. Review the three objectives identified previously (Prepare; Ensure; Communicate.)

2. Ask the Trainee questions such as the following in reference to the upcoming training event:

    a. "What appealed to you as you reviewed the background, objectives and targeted competencies for the program you are about to attend?"

    b. "How do you think attending this course could make a positive difference for the productivity of your team?"

    c. "With those thoughts in mind, what are your goals for attending?"

3. Ensure that the Trainee clearly understands the following expectations for their participation during the training (MOT2):

    a. While at training, the Trainee will not be expected to actively perform their normal role; their "job" is to learn as much as they can possibly learn.

    b. The Trainee should bring their completed MOT1 document with them to the training event. The intent is to keep the agreed-upon learning objectives front of mind during the training program.

    c. At the conclusion of the training program, the Trainee should complete MOT2 in their Action Plan in preparation for the post-training discussion with their NLM (MOT3).

If possible, schedule the post-training MOT3 discussion during MOT1. If a Trainee is aware that they will be held accountable for drafting and eventually articulating a targeted Action Plan to transform learning into actionable steps, there is a strong probability those expectations will translate to increased involvement and performance during the training event.

Which brings us back to Brinkerhoff (Figure 5). A well-executed MOT1 drives a well-executed MOT2. A well-executed MOT2 positions success in MOT3. Understanding this flow can and will motivate the Trainee to conscientiously complete any and all course-related pre-work.

The Trainee will not only pay attention during the program,

but will actively engage. They will challenge the instructor/ facilitator to ensure they understand the message and, much more importantly, how that message can be and has been implemented successfully. As they draft their MOT2 Action Plan, they will seek feedback from the facilitator and other participants to ensure the plan they are devising makes sense.

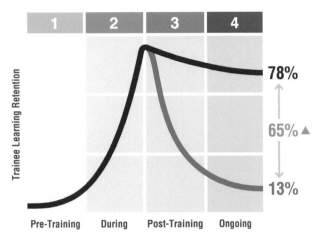

Figure 5: Positive impact due to Trainee accountability. (Adapted from Brinkerhoff RO, Apking AM. High Impact Learning: New Perspectives in Organizational Learning, Performance, and Change. Cambridge, MA: Perseus; 2001.)

And, one more time for the record: the NLM in no way, shape or form needs to be an expert in the subject matter covered in the training event. As evidence of that assertion, let's return to Sonya Carson. The most interesting aspect of her academic stewardship with young Ben? She couldn't read. Ponder that one for a minute or two.

Chapter 3: Key Takeaway

The NLM has significant potential to positively impact the outcomes of training. Can the spirit of Sonya Carson's twice-a-week essays be leveraged in any number of creative ways to connect what is learned with what is implemented on the job? In a word — absolutely! How much time should an NLM set aside to conduct a MOT1 coaching discussion? Approximately 15 focused minutes.

CHAPTER 4

MOT2: Maximum Engagement

Make no mistake about it, for any of the transfer strategies suggested in this or any other reference on sustainment to work, the training itself has to deliver. If the training is well-designed and relevant, Trainees have the potential to emerge from the event with a workable plan of action they can immediately set into motion. For that to occur at a very high level, the principles of adult learning must be on active display in the design of the learning, and if that learning is instructor-led, the Trainer also must be well-versed in the program's content while employing learner-centered platform skills throughout MOT2.

As we will review in some detail, the NLM needs to do all they can to communicate the importance of the training to all primary and secondary stakeholders. Beyond that, the NLM must take proactive steps to shield the Trainee from routine, day-to-day work-related responsibilities. But, when it comes right down to it, the outcome of MOT2 is primarily Trainee dependent. The Trainee has to put forth the effort and push themselves during the event. The NLM can take the actions identified in the last chapter to position success, but ultimately, the outcome of MOT2 is in the hands of the Trainee.

Key Questions

- ► How can NLMs unintentionally sabotage the transfer of training during the training event itself?

- ► What can Trainees do during formal learning to ensure they have a high probability of delivering on pre-established expectations for learning transfer?

THE FOUR MOMENTS *of* TRUTH™ | Next-Level Manager Guide

MOT2: Maximum Engagement
During Training

DIRECTIONS

☐ Reinforce to the Trainee your full commitment to their training experience and expectations for their active participation.

☐ Direct your team to minimize or eliminate interruptions for the Trainee to ensure their ability to fully engage in the training event.

☐ Remind the Trainee they will need to bring MOT1 to the training event to keep their goals for the training at the forefront of their mind.

☐ Refer to the MOT2 worksheet and direct the Trainee to bring it to the program as they will need to complete it immediately after training.

☐ Explain that they will use this information to develop their Action Plans and prepare for their MOT3 coaching discussion.

Notes

_____

_____

_____

_____

_____

_____

_____

_____

_____

_____

_____

_____

_____

_____

_____

MOT2 from the Situational Leadership®: Building Leaders 4MOT™ Next-Level Manager Guide.

It's analogous to the power each of us possesses anytime we decide to head to a fitness club for a workout. We can put our headphones on, wait for a treadmill or a stationary bike to open up, plug into the TV program or soundtrack of our choosing and go through the motions. Or, we can maximize our opportunity and find out what the slogan "no pain, no gain" really means! Head to any fitness club anywhere and you will see both ends of that spectrum and everything in between on active display.

MOT2: Maximum Engagement
During Training

DIRECTIONS

☐ Be sure to bring this MOT2 worksheet with you to the training so you can complete the learning summary below at the end of the program.

☐ Actively participate in training. Engage to the best of your ability and take personal responsibility to make this training a positive investment.

☐ At the end of training, complete the learning summary to document what you learned and how you plan to apply what you learned on the job.

☐ Refer to this information to develop your Action Plans for the MOT3 discussion with your NLM.

☐ Be prepared to share how your NLM can support your efforts and your progress.

Learning Summary

The three most important things I learned during the training are:

_____ _____ _____
_____ _____ _____
_____ _____ _____
_____ _____ _____
_____ _____ _____

This is how I plan to apply what I learned:

START DOING	STOP DOING	CONTINUE DOING
_____	_____	_____
_____	_____	_____
_____	_____	_____
_____	_____	_____
_____	_____	_____

5

MOT2 from the Situational Leadership®: Building Leaders 4MOT™ Trainee Guide.

Let's also readily acknowledge that any number of competing priorities and distractions exist that can send a Trainee with the best of intentions off track. At the absolute top of the list is the mobile device. Mobile technology provides 24/7/365 access to pretty much everything going on in the world, including minute-by-minute updates on the flow of business operations.

Ultimately, the degree to which Trainees allow interruptions/

updates to impact their focus during training is up to them. But, by the same token, there are expectations the NLM can publicize in advance that, at a minimum, will make their views on the absence of the Trainee explicit.

One suggestion for the Requiring Manager is to document their expectations for all to see and then be prepared to follow through, problem solve or prepare contingency plans as needed. Consider this hypothetical department/division memo as an example:

MEMO

FROM: Requiring Manager   **TO:** Department/Division

SUBJECT: Expectations Surrounding Company-Sponsored Training

Team, I know from personal experience how challenging it can be to step away from work to attend a training class or even to find dedicated, uninterrupted time to participate in online learning.

As I see it, when a member of our team attends training, their level of learning engagement is a product of how well the rest of us can fill in and provide cover until they get back to work. You just can't focus as well on learning something if you are trying to fulfill all of your responsibilities around here at the same time. So, my request is for your commitment to embrace the following expectations:

If you are scheduled to attend training, review your tasks and priorities for the time you will be unavailable and let the team and myself know how we can help you address those needs. Work together to prepare contingency plans for any surprises that you anticipate might pop up so we can manage those situations in your absence. I would like each of us to exercise discretion before calling, emailing or texting a teammate in training for a non-emergency. If you aren't sure whether a request or situation is an emergency, please reach out to me or another teammate to get a second opinion before interrupting.

When you are participating in online or virtual training, consider working from home to minimize distractions, and turn off email and messaging notifications while you are in an active session.

I am fully committed to supporting the investment each of you will make when attending training. My expectation is that each of you will hold yourselves accountable for taking advantage of these opportunities because they will help all of us learn, develop and improve. Please let me know if you have any concerns or questions about these expectations.

Thanks in advance for your commitment, and enjoy your training!

Sincerely,

NLM

Sample memo from Requiring Manager.

In reality, how many mangers send emails to their teams that resemble this one? Probably a precious few. On the other hand, how many would send and, more importantly, support the intention of a memo like this if someone in the training department effectively positioned the value of doing so and provided a template for them as a head start? Probably a whole lot more.

Trainee Engagement

As has been emphasized already, in addition to the NLM, the other key stakeholder in this equation is the learner, who bears personal responsibility for learning and developing an initial Action Plan to implement what has been learned during MOT2. This commitment to "learning engagement" fits somewhere under the much-publicized umbrella of all that is "employee engagement." Engagement, at a minimum, is an important barometer for company culture and a leading indicator for organizational productivity. If we acknowledge the mounds of data that suggest you can keep your job by consistently expending a mere 30 to 40 percent of your true potential, it stands to reason that significant gains can be realized by tapping into the remaining 60 to 70 percent of the available discretionary effort.

In response to those metrics, organizations implement one employee engagement initiative after another in a system-wide effort to turn those statistics around when it comes time to administer the next climate survey. And what has been the result of that effort so far? Not much change in the still depressingly low worldwide levels of employee engagement.

Like riding a roller coaster, the periodic organizational frenzy of implementing engagement initiatives based on climate surveys bears substantial similarity to the manner in which many training departments measure outcomes and subsequently make curriculum-based decisions. According to data, upwards of 95 percent of organizations that offer training conduct formal Level 1 evaluations. Less than one-third evaluate outcomes at Level 3. The extent of feedback-related curriculum decisions that many in the training community employ on the basis of minimal Level 1 feedback is striking. For example, how often might an activity in a program be discarded or a facilitator removed from future consideration because one or two learners marked the low end of their Likert scale on an end-of-course evaluation?

Similar to employee engagement, learner engagement is also a two-way street. Employees and learners are not innocent bystanders in the relationships they have with their employers or trainers. They are active participants with the potential to improve their situations, increase their own learning and exert positive influence on their peers and colleagues. When learners avoid opportunities to provide real-time feedback in favor of passively enduring an experience that turns out to be less than expected, they become part of the problem as opposed to the genesis of a viable solution. They also risk missing opportunities to ensure that they retain and sustain more of the learning gained in the training session.

Marshall Goldsmith serves as one of the first and best resources for exploring the notion of reciprocal employee engagement initiatives. In his best-selling book *"Triggers,"* and in the spirit of President Kennedy's famous challenge to the American people in the 1960s, he suggests:

"Ask not what your organization is doing to improve employee engagement; ask what you are doing to take responsibility to become more engaged."

He then goes on to list a series of simple questions anybody can ask themselves every day which actively place responsibility for contribution, progress and engagement squarely on the shoulders of the individual employee, regardless of their level in their organization's hierarchy. In that spirit, and with a focus on training, consider the following questions any Trainee could ask themselves during MOT1 in an effort to take full responsibility for getting the most out of any scheduled learning experience:

Will I do my best to ...
Prepare myself to learn?
Did I complete all of the required pre-work? Reach out to other learners that have taken this course? Contact the facilitator regarding expectations? Review and refine my Action Plan? Put some thought into what my participant introduction will be during the training program? Identify questions I need answered to help me prepare for my post-training discussion with my NLM?

Engage (early and often) throughout the course?
Am I prepared to introduce myself to others attending the training? Introduce myself to the facilitator? Complete each course activity to the best of my ability? Actively listen to the facilitator and peer learners? Recognize peer learners (publicly and one-on-one) when they say or do something that accelerates my learning?

Identify how I can help my team become more productive?
Are there things I am currently doing that I need to do more of? Things I need to stop doing? Things I am currently not doing that I need to start doing?

Build relationships with peer learners?
Which of my learning peers seem to have challenges and opportunities that are most closely aligned with mine? What can I learn from them? Which of my learning peers has challenges and

opportunities that I am not currently experiencing? What can I learn from them? Are any of my learning peers struggling? How can I help them?

Find meaning and help improve?
Is there anything I am learning that would help me with my family? My friends? Who else do I know who would benefit from this training? Why? Outside of completing the end-of-course evaluation, is there any feedback I could offer that might take a good program and help make it better?

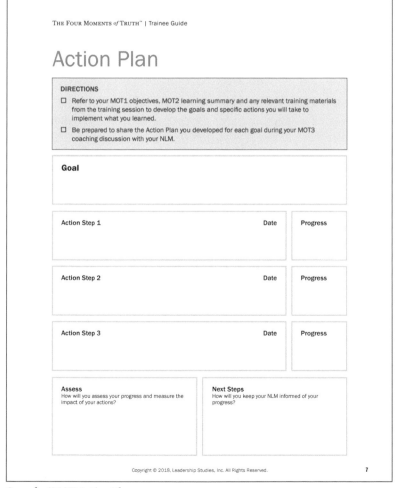

Sample 4MOT Action Plan.

Prepare for MOT3?
How can I apply what I have learned to improve the productivity of our team? What action(s) will I take? Who will be impacted by these actions? How will that impact be measured? What kind of support, guidance or autonomy will I need from my NLM? How long will it take to see tangible results?

Imagine a training experience where every learner, to the best of their ability, held themselves accountable for asking and answering each of these questions. What would that workshop be like? I would suggest that all of us have the potential to increase our levels of engagement exponentially when cast in the role of Trainee. And, if we commit to that proposition, we will wind up being the primary beneficiaries.

Case in point: I would imagine all of us can reflect on somebody we knew growing up who consistently practiced what this chapter has preached and subsequently experienced the benefits. Think back to your own educational experiences. Who was the best student you ever went to school with? For me, hands down, it was a guy named Frank Cardone. I attended El Segundo High School in the 1970s (Go Eagles!). I haven't seen Frank in over 40 years, but his approach to learning was like a "what good looks like" promo tape for *"Will I do my best to ...?"*

Frank was a straight-A student. As a matter of fact, it was a forgone conclusion that he was going to ace any class he took. I remember asking him one day how he did it. The following is a paraphrased account — from admittedly distant memory — but it was the kind of conversation that sticks with you for whatever crazy reason. One of my foremost memories about the exchange was how willing Frank was to share his "secrets." It was almost as if he was enjoying the fact that somebody had finally asked him about it:

"How do I get such good grades? You know the funny thing about it? Everybody thinks it's about how smart I am ... but the truth is ... 'smarts' has very little to do with it. I have a system, and I work that system every semester and with every class, starting with Day 1. The teacher passes out the syllabus for the class. Happens every time! That syllabus helps me sort of create my own map for each course. It tells me month by month, week by week, and class by class what's coming and when. That helps me plan my time so I can be sure to stay ahead of the pace. I don't know if you've ever noticed, but the first two weeks of every semester I am nowhere to be found. For the first two weeks, I stay up late, get up early, even on the weekends. I read every book and I complete every assignment. I get out in front, and I stay there. I'm not only one or two steps ahead of other students, I'm usually one or two steps ahead of every teacher."

I remember hearing this at age 17 or 18 and thinking it was both crazy and brilliant at the exact same time. I also remember getting answers to a number of questions that I didn't ask, such as:

- "Why wasn't Frank ever intimidated by all these random pop quizzes that came up out of nowhere?"

- "Why did it seem like the teacher's responses to Frank's classroom questions always seemed to start with: 'Frank, we'll be covering that in a week or two. But for now, simply focus on ...'"

As much as anyone I have ever come in direct contact with, Frank Cardone assumed personal responsibility for his own learning. I assume those habits were repeated or even upgraded a bit when he attended Stanford a few years later and undoubtedly went on to a ridiculously successful career.

My question after all this reflection and in the context of MOT2 is this: As learners, what the heck is preventing all of us from channeling our inner Frank Cardone and taking more control of our learning destiny? The answer I keep coming up with is — not much.

Chapter 4: Key Takeaway

4MOT™ (or for that matter, any system of training transfer) requires the training, whatever it may be, to be of high quality. The NLM plays a key role in ensuring Trainees enter training with a sense of purpose and are unencumbered by their ongoing, day-to-day work responsibilities (e.g., documented and published expectations sent to all regarding the availability of Trainees during a learning event). But ultimately, the Trainee bears significant personal responsibility for the success and effectiveness of the learning experience (i.e., Did the Trainee do their best to prepare, engage or find meaning?).

CHAPTER 5

MOT3: Perfect Practice

In MOT3, role emphasis shifts to the NLM. The knee-jerk approach many NLMs can have regarding the post-training MOT3 discussion is to overemphasize support, empowerment and active listening at the expense of becoming a driving and dedicated catalyst for a specific plan that has a high probability of producing sustained behavior change. It's human nature, to a degree. The Trainee is excited and has worked hard to put together their MOT2 plan during training. The NLM can very easily get swept up in this enthusiasm and wind up prematurely assigning responsibility for implementation to the Trainee without offering constructive and strategic evaluation and feedback.

With that perspective as a backdrop, consider an example of a MOT3 exchange that leaves room for significant improvement on the part of the NLM. Let's assume the Trainee has successfully completed their 4MOT™ Action Plan, as instructed.

Key Questions

▶ What (in specific terms) are the changes in behavior the Trainee intends to implement on the job as a result of experiences in the formal learning event?

▶ What are the anticipated results the Trainee expects to see as a result of these changes?

▶ How will those results be measured?

▶ What role does the Trainee see the NLM playing as the Trainee implements the proposed changes in behavior (e.g., directive, collaborative, empowering)?

Now, assume there is a scheduled MOT3 meeting between the Trainee and the NLM shortly after training has been completed, which plays out something like this:

Example 1

NLM: "I'm looking forward to hearing what you learned in training, and I suppose I am even more interested to hear how you plan to implement what you learned."

Trainee: "First off, what a great program! Thanks for giving me the opportunity to attend."

NLM: "I'm glad you enjoyed the experience. I had a feeling you would. (Perusing MOT3 Action Plan) It certainly looks as though you have given this quite a bit of thought, and I appreciate that! Walk me through what you came up with."

Trainee: "OK, well, as you can see, the first thing I came to grips with was ..."

The Trainee reviews the documented plan in detail, and the NLM periodically interjects with catch phrases such as, "I like that," or "I hadn't thought of that." As the meeting concludes ...

NLM: "I'm really impressed with the plan! I'm excited to see where this takes you, and I have every reason to share your optimism. A couple of your completion dates are a bit optimistic, so let's monitor your progress and recalibrate if need be."

Trainee: "Sounds good."

NLM: "And, as always, if you 'hit a wall' or find yourself getting off track for whatever reason, let me know."

Trainee: "Will do!"

In all likelihood, both parties will leave this discussion feeling positive and satisfied. Exchanges like this are similar to the well-intentioned acquaintance at the end-of-year holiday party who articulates, with clear conviction, their New Year's weight-loss resolution to whomever happens to be within earshot. There is passion; there is faith; there is an articulated vision of behavior change. In return, there is positive reinforcement, encouragement and support. Unfortunately, there is also a 92 percent probability that the plan will be a distant memory by Super Bowl Sunday.

MOT3 is not an artificial opportunity for the NLM to practice the power of positivity. Rather, it is a crucial interlude where the two parties actively negotiate the parameters of a personalized change initiative. That plan needs to account for obstacles that neither party can accurately predict but that both parties must proactively acknowledge, account for and address. The bottom-line reason Level 1 and Level 2 outcomes correlate in no way with Level 3 outcomes is that, typically, no bridge exists between the learning event and the iterative nature of real-world behavior change. Understanding what you need to do is completely different than actually doing it.

During MOT3, the NLM serves as the bridge between the Trainee's newfound knowledge and the development of observable skills. To be effective, the NLM doesn't necessarily need to attend the training in question, but they do need to be conversant in the language of the training received. At CLS, we supply each NLM with a coaching guide that includes key takeaways and discussion questions for each program we offer. Here are examples taken from our *Situational Leadership®: Building Leaders* program:

DISCUSSION QUESTIONS

☐ What were the three most important things you learned?

☐ In specific terms, how do you plan to implement what you learned to the benefit of our team?

☐ How will we measure the impact of that implementation?

☐ Tell me how I can help (e.g., provide support, guidance or give autonomy).

The intent of these references is to help the NLM prepare for a meaningful exchange that charts a course for training-based behavior change and performance improvement. At some juncture during MOT3, that exchange needs to include transparent acknowledgement, pre-emptive planning and targeted coaching in the pursuit of iterative progress.

THE FOUR MOMENTS *of* TRUTH™ | Next-Level Manager Guide

MOT3: Perfect Practice
Post-Training Coaching
(one to two weeks after training)

DIRECTIONS

☐ Review the goals and action steps the Trainee developed on their Action Plans.

☐ Provide feedback and coaching to make any necessary adjustments.

☐ Gain alignment with your Trainee regarding expectations for next steps (e.g., ongoing touchpoints or status updates; the role you should play in goal achievement; etc.).

☐ Schedule the MOT4 discussion.

Notes

DISCUSSION QUESTIONS

• What were the three most important things you learned?

• In specific terms, how do you plan to implement what you learned to the benefit of our team?

• How will we measure the impact of that implementation?

• Tell me how I can help (e.g., provide support, guidance or give autonomy)

MOT3 instructions for the Next-Level Manager.

Now imagine how different the exchange would be between our hypothetical Trainee and NLM if the NLM were able to apply a structured process to gain mutual task alignment and accountability:

Example 2

NLM: "I genuinely want to thank you for the obvious effort you put into preparing for and participating in training. It is clear from the plan that you have put together that you took this seriously and recognize how putting elements of what you learned into practice can help us all. Much appreciated!"

Trainee: "Thank you! I'm excited to take action on all of this."

NLM: "Good! And I would be remiss if I didn't provide a little perspective grounded in my experience with these matters."

Trainee: "Great!"

NLM: "In general, I want to take a critical look at your Action Plan for each goal. I want to see if we can fine-tune the plan at least a little, make it more specific and put some proactive thought into what could go wrong or get you derailed and factor that in. I suppose, more than anything, I would feel terrible if all the obvious work you have put into this didn't translate, almost immediately, into some noticeable impact. So, I'd like to figure out how I can play more of a role, at least early on, to monitor your progress, provide ongoing feedback and ensure you are moving in the right direction. Consider me like a personal trainer for a fitness goal in that regard."

Trainee: "OK."

Now, I can only imagine that many will read that simulated narrative and ask, "What world are you living in? Do you honestly expect NLMs to sign on as personal trainers for every direct report they have who goes through training?" The short answer I would give to those questions is a qualified, "YES!" If the training cost is justified under the premise that learning what is taught and implementing that newly acquired knowledge will tangibly contribute to improved performance, then that is exactly what should be expected. Further, I would suggest that there are organizations that make, or at least have made over the years, those NLM expectations explicit. In so doing, they have actually leveraged training as a legitimate competitive advantage (e.g., Deloitte, Merck, Procter & Gamble, Amgen, IBM and many more). That competitive advantage initiates with MOT3 when Trainees emerge from training and find out if what they learned is valued by their organizational culture and, as such, is a priority for their NLM.

This brings us back to the notion Dr. Hersey offered years ago:

**"Practice ... does not make perfect;
perfect practice ... makes perfect!"**

Let's take a minute to unpack that notion. Many in our field have identified, in a variety of different ways, how easy behavior change is to understand and how frustratingly difficult it is to achieve. For example, this view was brought to center stage a few years back by Malcolm Gladwell in his best-selling treatise *"Outliers."* One of the most intriguing chapters in that book was entitled "10,000 Hours." It was based on research compiled by Dr. Anders Ericsson that tackles the myth that great achievement is a function of unique talent. Dr. Ericsson's career, which began at Carnegie Mellon University in the late 1970s and is still going strong today at Florida State University, provides compelling evidence that extraordinary performance is a function of what he refers to as "deliberate practice."

Chronicled in his recent book *"PEAK: Secrets From the New Science of Expertise,"* Dr. Ericsson provides example after example from the fields of athletics, music, chess, typing, calculation, memory/cognitive skills and more to prove the point that practice does not make perfect, but perfect practice can and quite often does. Here are the elements of perfect practice as identified by Dr. Ericsson:

Specific Goals

Perfect practice commences with measurable, progressive targets. Performance improvement is based on iterative progress and successive approximation, which is, in essence, a trend line of performance that skews upward and to the right. Each iteration is benchmarked off the previously established performance peak. In the context of the 4MOT, NLMs need to help Trainees take general goals and break them down into their most fundamental elements so the Trainees can work on each with a realistic expectation of improvement. In "training speak," it's where "the 70 becomes tangibly integrated with the 10" (i.e., on-the-job requirements are integrated with the formal learning event). The NLM, armed with information about the intent of the training, such as objectives and targeted competencies, is uniquely positioned to identify elements of job performance that serve as real-world role-play opportunities.

Focused Attention

I had a basketball coach named Bill Rayl (about 40 pounds and 40 years ago) who used to routinely challenge us during timeouts in closely contested games by saying (or sometimes screaming), "YOU GOTTA WANT THIS!" When it comes to achieving Level 3 outcomes or accomplishing pretty much anything of significance in life, truer words were never spoken. If the Trainee has no real desire to improve, there is very little the NLM can do to force the issue. There were a number of participants in Dr. Ericsson's research over the years who lacked the necessary level of achievement orientation to qualify as a peak performer. Along the very same lines for the 4MOT or any other system dedicated to the transfer of training to work, the Trainee has, in the words of coach Rayl, "GOTTA WANT TO IMPROVE!" Talking about your desire to lose weight next year at a holiday party is one thing; acting on that by getting out of bed before work each day to exercise in mid-January and beyond is a different thing altogether. At a minimum, during MOT3, NLMs need to tactfully identify these distinctions.

Feedback

When it comes to putting newly acquired knowledge into active practice, Trainees need to understand when they are doing something right and, perhaps even more importantly, when and what they are doing wrong. Feedback is the tool NLMs can leverage to accelerate the development of their direct reports and redirect any performance-related regression.

Accelerating development is a function of honest, objective, performance-based discussion. NLMs need to know how to engage in those discussions, and Trainees need to know how to receive and implement the suggestions offered. If nothing else, MOT3 provides a structured and targeted opportunity for NLMs to reiterate performance expectations.

Get Out of Your Comfort Zone

This premise of getting out of your comfort zone lies at the foundation of change at any level. For our purposes here and in alignment with effectively providing feedback, the Trainee needs to be willing to trust. They need to trust the notion that what they learned in training works not only in a classroom setting, but also on the job. They need to trust that the NLM has the best interests of both productivity and the Trainee's personal development in mind. They need to be open to new ideas an NLM may have about trying differently rather than trying harder. Throughout the years, I have had many opportunities to ask learners to think about the best manager they ever had and identify what made that particular manager stand out. The answer I have heard most frequently could be paraphrased as follows:

> "She was tough, by no means easy to work for. I really didn't fully appreciate the impact she had on my career until I had been promoted. At the end of the day, I think it really boiled down to the fact that, at the time, she had higher expectations for me than I had for myself. She simply wouldn't allow me to fall short of my full potential."

MOT3 is the intersection of learning and performance coaching.

If all goes well during the training event itself, the Trainee shows up to MOT3 with fresh knowledge and strong desire. The NLM needs to be prepared to fan that flame and act as a catalyst in the Trainee's journey to achieve their full potential — whether the Trainee realizes that's what's going on at the time or not!

Chapter 5: Key Takeaways

Practice in and of itself does not make perfect. The impact associated with a Trainee practicing something learned in training is a function of goal setting, dedicated repetition, accurate measurement and ongoing feedback. In other words, the Trainee and the NLM work together to develop the routines of perfect practice.

CHAPTER 6

MOT4: Performance Support

A well-executed and intentional MOT3 discussion is designed to successfully facilitate a seamless transition to MOT4 and continued coaching. This typically occurs two to three months after the training and MOT3. By that time, the Trainee should have had an opportunity not only to implement the Action Plan, but to have seen initial results. From this point forward, the focus is on measuring and monitoring performance. This translates to the Trainee and the NLM performing the following key tasks:

- Documenting progress and discussing emergent challenges
- Updating the Action Plan as needed
- Determining if additional support is needed

In short, MOT4 is the intersection of learning support and performance support in the form of ongoing coaching.

Cultural Alignment

The central theme of this book is that behavior change doesn't just happen. That is particularly the case with behavior change that discernibly impacts productivity. Behavior change is iterative. It is a function of trial, error, setbacks, progress, reinforcement and encouragement. Once again, with bias duly noted, I would offer that when a training program simply doesn't work, it may

Key Questions
- What are the design-related implications of developing training that is intentionally anchored in NLM reinforcement and on-the-job performance?

have much more to do with the stakeholders and the culture surrounding the training than it does with the training itself.

This brings to mind a number of opportunities I have had over the years to work with industry-leading sales organizations. I learned very quickly that most sales professionals in no way struggle when it comes time to speak their minds. As an external, third-party consultant, I found I could usually assess the relationship between the field sales organization and the marketing division very quickly. When that relationship was out of sync, I would frequently hear comments from sales types such as:

> "Between you and me, I have no idea sometimes what our marketing people are thinking or where they are getting their information. But I can tell you this with a high degree of certainty, it clearly isn't from us or from our customers."

This could be followed by an exchange like this:

> "Perfect example right here (thrusts a one-page promotional piece across the table). That's a sales aid I am supposed to be discussing with my customers on upcoming calls. I have no idea where the data came from or what the conclusions are supposed to mean. But I can promise you this, if I marched up to the customers that truly drive revenue in my territory and walked through that thing (points to the promotional piece), they would laugh me out of their office, wonder what in the world was wrong with me or both!"

What does that hypothetical narrative have to do with the transfer of training? Effective marketing teams intentionally work through the sales team as they craft messages and campaigns intended to influence their customers. They recognize the power that individual sales representatives have to pull through their marketing initiatives or ensure they "die on the vine." This is much the same with effective training teams, Trainees and NLMs. If the NLM can truly make or break the bottom-line impact of a training

MOT4: Performance Support

Ongoing Coaching
(three months after training)

DIRECTIONS

☐ By this three-month discussion, the Trainee should have had an opportunity to implement the Action Plans developed in MOT3.

☐ Discuss progress toward goals.

☐ Update the Action Plans, as necessary, and establish next steps to continue the Trainee's progress toward goal achievement.

☐ Provide ongoing coaching to reinforce the application of new skills and knowledge.

Notes

DISCUSSION QUESTIONS

- What has been working?
- What specific progress have you made against your goals?
- What has gotten in your way?
- How, if at all, do we need to adjust our plan moving forward?

7

MOT4 instructions for the Next-Level Manager.

program, then the training function/team should clearly do everything they can to make sure NLMs are passionately aligned with the training intervention long before it gets rolled out. Let's take one more walk down memory lane to illustrate that point.

Years ago, I had the distinct honor to engage in leadership development work with an industry-leading pharmaceutical company. Everything about them was creative, innovative and trendsetting, from the products they developed to the people they hired and the standards they set. Consistent with those norms, they recognized the need to hire a Director of Sales Training and task that individual with designing, developing, delivering and evaluating a cutting-edge sales training program. They engaged in an extensive search that took over nine months. The person they hired was one of the smartest training people I have ever met. The breadth and depth of his familiarity with adult learning, instructional design principles and evaluation technique was beyond impressive.

As he embarked upon developing the sales training program he was hired to create, he assembled his team and conducted comprehensive research. Under his direction, his team conducted skills assessments, competency analyses, best-practice exploration and expansive content reviews. He likened the process his team undertook to that of the research scientists this pharmaceutical company employed to investigate disease entities, study complex molecules and then emerge from the laboratory with a viable therapy that was ready to endure the rigors of FDA trials.

After a little over 18 months, the program was unveiled. The results? Think Charles Dickens and *"A Tale of Two Cities"*: "It was the best of times; it was the worst of times."

First, the good news. The training community loved literally everything about this program. This individual, along with various members of his team, were asked to present at multiple training conferences showcasing this cutting-edge selling skills masterpiece. They outlined the process the team followed. They detailed how the objectives of the program were seamlessly integrated with the evaluation strategy. They defined what novice, intermediate and mastery levels of performance for each competency looked like. They fielded questions from others at these conferences regarding the best practices that had been identified and any advice this team may have for others in the audience with similar aspirations in support of their own organizations.

The Dickensian tragedy associated with this masterpiece? It was never really implemented. There were a few — very few — sales regions that scheduled delivery. Those sessions received mixed reviews at best. The biggest part of the problem was that, after waiting 18 months for rollout, those attending were expecting some sort of career-changing, transformational event. What they got was a really good program that shed some interesting light on the fundamentals of effective customer influence, which most were familiar with already.

Beyond that, and with the benefit of a long, clear look into the rearview mirror, the reason that award-winning program was a huge internal bust had everything to do with lack of NLM support. By the time this program became available, NLMs, almost across the board, had become alienated, disenfranchised and rebellious. With all of the analysis that had taken place in the training laboratory over the 18 months of development, little time, if any, had been spent on field rides with company sales professionals or collaborative exchanges with NLMs. Many of those NLMs had informally developed their own selling skills training and justified doing so in a variety of different ways:

> "Am I supposed to wait around for two years and do nothing while the training department completes the dissertation that will unveil how our reps are supposed to approach our customers?"

As I hope this example suggests, and as I am confident you already know, effective training design is truly an inclusive process. Philosophically, a needs assessment should be viewed as an extended, investigative sales call performed by the training function and intended to build credibility with NLMs.

- ▸ "Here are your roadblocks. Agree?"
- ▸ "Here's how training can help you 'bust through' or 'navigate around' those obstacles. Agree?"
- ▸ "Here's what we plan to develop. Agree?"
- ▸ "Here's what I need from you to make this work (MOT1 to MOT4)."

Net-net, the training function needs to begin the design process with MOT4 and work backwards. It may be more complex than it sounds, but the benefits associated with initiating design and development efforts in active collaboration with NLMs would be well worth the effort, particularly when focused on finding practical answers to questions such as:

> "How do current on-the-job requirements (that NLMs coach to each and every day) integrate with what is being learned in training?"

In training speak, that question would suggest that we:

1. Start with job requirements that truly drive productivity (i.e., "the 70 percent").

2. Design and develop formal training that accelerates targeted growth (i.e., "the 10 percent").

3. Recognize the power the NLM has with each Trainee to assimilate "the 70 with the 10."

In the context of the "training as change" graphic introduced in Chapter 2, and in the words of James Kirkpatrick:

"You need to start with the flag at the top of the mountain and work your way backwards."

If you start with the flag at the top of the mountain, the cascade of questions and subsequent thoughtful answers flow rather naturally:

- "What does productivity really look like?"
  - "Strategic objectives that, if achieved, will improve competitive standing"
- "What do employees at all levels need to be doing to hit those productivity targets?"
  - "What are the key behaviors that produce the most important results?"
    - "If we are currently exhibiting those behaviors, how do we reinforce those actions and keep doing what we're doing?"
    - "If we aren't, what do we need to start doing or stop doing to get (and keep) ourselves on track?"
- "What does training look like that teaches/promotes the behaviors we need to see in order to produce the results we need to achieve?"
  - "Who are the key stakeholders who will ensure our investment in formal learning is directly connected to on-the-job performance and the achievement of important results?"
  - "How do we ensure our formal learning is both relevant and engaging?"

Clearly, this is only a partial list of the applicable inquiries that need to be considered. Also, I am confident it reads (to the seasoned training professional) as common sense. But, as previously mentioned, all too often, common sense does not readily translate to common practice. Recent research suggests that 90 to 95 percent of training design and development efforts remain focused upon the learning event, despite all we know about the disconnect between Level 2 and Level 3 outcomes.

If you want "a seat at the big table" as a training professional, if you want to find meaning in your role, add measurable value and truly matter, ensure you are spending 50 percent of your time focused on the requirements, needs and behavior changing potential of the NLMs in your organization.

For what it is worth, at CLS, we include the 4MOT™ with every course offering we market — free of charge. And, lest you attribute that to a passion for unbridled altruism, I feel compelled to extend a disclaimer. Clearly, CLS benefits when our formal learning is joined at the hip with positive outcomes defined by a variety of metrics. Simply stated, we definitely have "skin in the game!"

Even if you have no intention of investing in Situational Leadership® training, I offer the Four Moments of Truth™ on behalf of all of us at The Center for Leadership Studies. It is a mechanism of training transfer that can serve as a bridge between effective training of any kind, behavior change grounded in that learning experience and results that prove, as a learning professional, you do indeed matter!

In closing, and on behalf of all the dedicated professionals at CLS, sincere thanks for taking time out of what I know is a demanding schedule to become more familiar with the Four Moments of Truth. Do not hesitate to call or contact us and provide us with the opportunity to practice what has been preached!

Afterword

Doug Harward

The goal of any leader of a training organization is to align the training activities to the needs of the business. This, in turn, provides for the development of employees and/or clients to perform at a level necessary for the business to prosper.

To achieve this objective, there are many strategies used to create interactive and engaging content or to leverage technologies to improve the access to courseware. For many years, the most common strategy used by corporate training organizations was to simulate an academic institution by operating as a school within the business. This approach is referred to as a "corporate university." A host of courses are offered whereby the learner has the autonomy to choose the course that best meets their needs and registers themselves when the course availability aligns with their work schedule. We called this an event-based, supply-oriented model for corporate training. Unfortunately, this model has not fared well with corporate executives, leaving many questions about the efficacy and return on investment.

Comparing this model to the most noted scientific research about how we best learn and develop skills, we find there is much we can do to transform training from an events-based model to one based on modern learning system practices. Modern learning systems, as noted in research by Training Industry, Inc., is founded on principles developed over many years by the world's leading psychologists and learning theorists. These principles provide valuable insights into how we best learn and retain information, as well as how we develop behaviors that evolve into expert performance.

For example, in the late 1800s, Dr. Hermann Ebbinghaus found that memory is enhanced when we absorb information over an extended period of time. His theory of the "spacing effect" was instrumental in teaching us that conscious competence increases when information is consumed and repeated over time, improving our ability to apply information much more effectively.

In the mid-1900s, Dr. B.F. Skinner expanded this research to help us understand the effects of positive and negative reinforcement as a means of conditioning behavior. He helped us understand that we could affect behavior by controlling the type of reinforcement (positive verses negative) that was offered. This also helped us understand much about the relationship between learning and behavior.

More recent and ongoing research around performance is being done by Dr. Anders Ericsson (mentioned in Chapter 5). Dr. Ericsson studies some of the world's most respected experts in various fields such as medicine, music and athletics. He has found they achieved a high level of performance by being intentional and deliberate about how they approached improvement. He calls this approach "deliberate practice." He helps us understand that knowledge by itself does not imply an ability to perform. High levels of performance comes from our ability to apply knowledge learned in structured training to day-to-day tasks and behaviors while doing a job.

Creating a training program that helps learners reach an expert level of performance requires us to focus on several aspects of the learning experience. First, when designing training, we should think of designing a learning experience as opposed to designing just a course. The experience includes all the aspects of learning and behavior improvement, from what occurs before the course as well as after the course is completed. We call this the extended learning experience and it includes a series of activities surrounding the event such as pre-course preparation and post-course practice and reinforcement. Designing an extended learning experience highly increases the probability of true behavior improvement.

Second, the experience must include how a learner gets access to feedback as they progress up the learning curve. Feedback obviously provides proper direction of how to change from previous mistakes and reinforces when something is done correctly. The most important feedback is that which the learner provides themselves. Greatest personal improvement comes when a learner consciously understands their own behavioral needs and can evaluate their own performance, and then adjust and learn from their mistakes. An example is when a basketball player shoots a free throw. They immediately know if the shot goes in the basket or not. This immediate feedback provides them information they can use to improve.

Thirdly, the intentional involvement of a coach throughout the process keeps the learner in line with objectives and job expectations and provides direction and ideas for how to improve. Dr. Ericsson has found that those who perform at the highest levels recognize they could not have achieved success without the direction and support of their coach.

The 4MOT™ is an exceptional approach that utilizes these strategies to provide an innovative and, most importantly, effective way to develop leaders. It applies the scientifically proven principles that include involvement of the coach or supervisor throughout the learning experience. And, it ensures that good behavior is reinforced and methods for improvement are a part of the coach's objectives. The 4MOT takes a stakeholder's perspective to training design. Learning experience design includes all stakeholders and their role in the learning process — not just the learners. It includes a direct focus on the course materials as well as the roles the learner, facilitator and coach play during the learning experience.

In corporate training speak, the 4MOT extends the learning experience and provides a methodology for how we best achieve the highest level of performance, whether it be for leaders, factory workers, sales professionals or virtually anyone in the enterprise.

References

1. ASTD Research Study (2009). *The Value of Evaluation: Making Training Evaluations More Effective.* Alexandria, VA: American Society for Training and Development.

2. Brinkerhoff RO, Apking AM. *High Impact Learning: New Perspectives in Organizational Learning, Performance, and Change.* Cambridge, MA: Perseus; 2001.

3. Brinkerhoff RO. *The Success Case Method: Find Out Quickly What's Working and What's Not.* San Francisco, CA: Berrett-Koehler Publishers; 2003.

4. Brinkerhoff RO. *Telling Training's Story: Evaluation Made Simple, Credible, and Effective.* San Francisco, CA: Berrett-Koehler Publishers; 2006.

5. Broad ML, Newstrom JW, *Transfer of Training: Action Packed Strategies to Ensure High Payoff From Training Investments.* Perseus Publishing; 1992.

6. Carson B. *Gifted Hands: The Ben Carson Story.* Grand Rapids, MI: Zondervan; 2011.

7. Ericsson A, Pool R. *PEAK: Secrets From the New Science of Expertise.* New York, NY: Houghton Mifflin Harcourt Publishing Company; 2016.

8. Gladwell M. *Outliers: The Story of Success.* Columbus, GA: Little, Brown and Company; 2008.

9. Goldsmith M. *Triggers: Creating Behavior That Lasts — Becoming the Person You Want to Be.* New York, NY: Crown Business; 2015.

10. Kirkpatrick DL, Kirkpatrick JD. *Evaluating Training Programs: The Four Levels.* 3rd ed. San Francisco, CA: Berrett-Koehler Publishers, Inc.; 2006.

11. Kirkpatrick JD, Kirkpatrick WK. *Kirkpatrick's Four Levels of Training Evaluation.* Arlington, VA: ATD Press; 2016.

About the Author

Dr. Sam Shriver is the Executive Vice President of Research and Development at The Center for Leadership Studies (CLS). In that capacity, he serves as a senior thought leader, subject matter expert and author. Sam has over 35 years of direct experience with Situational Leadership®, organizational behavior and leadership development.

He holds a B.S. from the U.S. Coast Guard Academy and an MBA from Pepperdine University, and he earned his Ed.D. in training and development from North Carolina State University.

Sam has designed and developed over 200 custom leadership and coaching programs and has been formally recognized by Bernsin, Brandon Hall and the Association for Talent Development (ATD) in that regard. He has also authored numerous training and development white papers, journal articles and blogs, in addition to the book and audio series, *"From Coach to Coach."* He has also coauthored a best-selling service quality improvement program, Frontline Service.

About The Center for Leadership Studies

For more than 50 years, The Center for Leadership Studies, founded by Dr. Paul Hersey, has been the global home of the original Situational Leadership® Model. With over 14 million leaders trained, Situational Leadership® is the most successful and widely adopted leadership model available. Deployed in more than 70 percent of Fortune 500 companies, our Situational Leadership® Model and influence-focused courses enable leaders to engage in effective performance conversations that build trust, increase productivity and drive behavior change. CLS services customers both domestically and internationally through an extensive network comprised of over 200 learning professionals in more than 25 languages.

At The Center for Leadership Studies, We Build Leaders and Drive Behavior Change.

www.situational.com

919.335.8763